gourmet Burgers

and magnificent sides

Publications International, Ltd.

Microwave Cooking: Microwave ovens vary in wattage. Use the cooking times as guidelines and check for doneness before adding more time.

Preparation/Cooking Times: Preparation times are based on the approximate amount of time required to assemble the recipe before cooking, baking, chilling or serving. These times include preparation steps such as measuring, chopping and mixing. The fact that some preparations and cooking can be done simultaneously is taken into account. Preparation of optional ingredients and serving suggestions is not included.

Publications International, Ltd.

Table of Contents

Great Grilled Burgers with Spinach Pesto

    Spinach Pesto (recipe follows)
1½ pounds ground beef chuck
  ¼ teaspoon salt
  ¼ teaspoon black pepper
  4 to 8 slices provolone cheese
  4 crusty Italian rolls, split and toasted
    Tomato slices
    Oak leaf lettuce

1. Prepare grill for direct cooking. Prepare Spinach Pesto.

2. Combine beef, ¼ cup pesto, salt and pepper in large bowl; mix lightly. Shape into 4 patties about ¾ inch thick. Reserve remaining pesto.

3. Grill patties over medium heat, covered, 8 to 10 minutes (or 13 to 15 minutes uncovered) to medium (160°F) or to desired doneness, turning once. Top burgers with cheese during last 2 minutes of grilling.

4. Spread remaining pesto on cut sides of each roll. Place burgers on bottom halves of rolls; top with tomato, lettuce and top halves of rolls.

Makes 4 servings

Spinach Pesto: Combine 2 cups spinach leaves, 3 tablespoons grated Romano cheese, 3 tablespoons olive oil, 1 tablespoon dried basil, 1 tablespoon lemon juice and 3 cloves garlic in food processor or blender; process until smooth. Makes about ½ cup.

Classic California Burgers

2 tablespoons *French's®* Honey Dijon Mustard
2 tablespoons mayonnaise
2 tablespoons sour cream
1 pound ground beef
2 tablespoons *French's®* Worcestershire Sauce
1⅓ cups *French's®* Cheddar or Original French Fried Onions, divided
½ teaspoon garlic salt
¼ teaspoon ground black pepper
4 hamburger rolls, split and toasted
½ small avocado, sliced
½ cup sprouts

1. Combine mustard, mayonnaise and sour cream; set aside.

2. Combine beef, Worcestershire, ⅔ *cup* French Fried Onions and seasonings. Form into 4 patties. Grill over high heat until juices run clear (160°F internal temperature).

3. Place burgers on rolls. Top each with mustard sauce, avocado slices, sprouts and remaining onions, dividing evenly. Cover with top halves of rolls.   *Makes 4 servings*

BBQ Cheese Burgers: Top each burger with 1 slice American cheese, 1 tablespoon barbecue sauce and 2 tablespoons French Fried Onions.

Pizza Burgers: Top each burger with pizza sauce, mozzarella cheese and French Fried Onions.

Prep Time: **10 minutes** | Cook Time: **10 minutes**

Classic California Burger

Bacon and Blue Cheese Stuffed Burgers

    4 slices applewood smoked bacon or regular bacon
    1 small red onion, finely chopped
    2 tablespoons crumbled blue cheese
    1 tablespoon butter, softened
  1½ pounds ground beef
       Salt and black pepper
    4 onion or plain hamburger rolls
       Lettuce leaves

1. Cook bacon in large skillet over medium-high heat until chewy. Drain on paper towels; chop into small pieces. Add onion to same skillet; cook until tender. Cool slightly.

2. Combine bacon, onion, blue cheese and butter in small bowl; mix well. Prepare grill for direct cooking.

3. Divide ground beef into 8 balls. Flatten each ball into thin patties about 4 inches wide; season with salt and pepper. Place 2 tablespoons bacon mixture in center of one patty; cover with second patty. Pinch edges together to seal. Repeat with remaining patties and cheese mixture.

4. Grill patties over medium heat, covered, 8 to 10 minutes (or 13 to 15 minutes uncovered) to medium (160°F) or until desired doneness, turning once. Transfer burgers to platter; let stand 2 minutes before serving. Serve burgers on rolls with lettuce.   *Makes 4 servings*

> **❚ TIP:** If you want juicy, flavorful burgers, do not flatten patties while grilling. Pressing down on the patties with a spatula not only squeezes out tasty juices, but in this recipe might also cause the stuffing to pop out.

Bacon and Blue Cheese Stuffed Burger

One-Bite Burgers

1 package (11 ounces) refrigerated breadstick dough
    (12 breadsticks)
1 pound ground beef
2 teaspoons hamburger seasoning mix
9 slices Cheddar or American cheese, quartered (optional)
36 round dill pickle slices
    Ketchup and mustard

1. Preheat oven to 375°F. Separate dough into 12 breadsticks; cut each breadstick into 3 equal pieces. Working with 1 piece at a time, tuck ends under to meet at center, pressing to seal and form very small bun about 1½ inches in diameter and ½ inch high.

2. Place buns seam side down on ungreased baking sheet. Bake 11 to 14 minutes or until golden brown. Remove to wire racks to cool.

3. Meanwhile, gently mix ground beef and seasoning in large bowl. Shape beef mixture into 36 patties, using about 2 teaspoons beef per patty.

4. Heat large skillet over medium heat. Cook patties 7 to 8 minutes or until cooked through, turning once. Top burgers with cheese, if desired.

5. Split buns in half crosswise. Place burgers on bottom halves of buns; top with pickle slices, ketchup, mustard and top halves of buns.

Makes 36 mini burgers

One-Bite Burgers

Parmesan Honey Lager Burgers

1½ pounds ground beef
¾ cup honey lager, divided
⅓ cup grated Parmesan cheese
1 tablespoon Worcestershire sauce
¼ teaspoon black pepper
3 tablespoons mayonnaise
3 tablespoons ketchup
½ teaspoon yellow mustard
8 tomato slices
8 red onion slices
4 hamburger buns

1. Prepare grill for direct cooking.

2. Combine beef, ¼ cup lager, Parmesan, Worcestershire sauce and pepper in large bowl; mix lightly. Shape into 4 patties. Combine 1 tablespoon lager, mayonnaise, ketchup and mustard in small bowl; set aside.

3. Grill patties over medium-high heat 3 minutes; turn and brush with some of remaining lager. Grill 3 minutes; turn and brush with lager. Repeat grilling and brushing 3 more times or until burgers are cooked to medium (160°F) or to desired doneness.

4. Place tomatoes, onions and burgers on bottom halves of buns; top with mayonnaise mixture and top halves of buns. Serve immediately.

Makes 4 servings

Parmesan Honey Lager Burger

Western Barbecue Burgers with Beer Barbecue Sauce

1½ pounds ground beef
1 cup smokehouse-style barbecue sauce
¼ cup brown ale
½ teaspoon salt
¼ teaspoon black pepper
1 red onion, cut into ½-inch-thick slices
4 hamburger buns
8 thick slices bacon, cooked until crisp
Lettuce leaves
Tomato slices

1. Prepare grill for direct cooking. Shape beef into 4 patties about ¾ inch thick. Cover and refrigerate.

2. Combine barbecue sauce, ale, salt and pepper in small saucepan. Bring mixture to boil; boil 1 minute. Remove from heat.

3. Grill onion slices over medium-high heat 4 minutes or until softened and slightly charred, turning occasionally. Grill patties, covered, 8 to 10 minutes (or 13 to 15 minutes uncovered) to medium (160°F) or to desired doneness, turning once.

4. Place burgers on bottom halves of buns; top with onion, bacon and barbecue sauce. Place lettuce and tomatoes on top halves of buns.

Makes 4 servings

Western Barbecue Burger with Beer Barbecue Sauce

Audacious Two-Cheese Burgers

1½ pounds ground beef chuck
⅓ cup chopped parsley
1 tablespoon Dijon mustard
1 tablespoon Worcestershire sauce
¾ teaspoon black pepper, divided
½ teaspoon dried thyme
½ thinly sliced English cucumber
3 slices red onion, separated into rings
4 radishes, thinly sliced
1 tablespoon olive oil
1 teaspoon red wine vinegar
¼ teaspoon salt
4 slices Cheddar cheese
4 slices Gouda cheese
Lettuce leaves
4 whole wheat rolls, split and toasted
Ketchup

1. Prepare grill for direct cooking. Combine beef, parsley, mustard, Worcestershire sauce, ½ teaspoon pepper and thyme in large bowl; mix lightly. Shape into 4 patties about ¾ inch thick. Cover and refrigerate.

2. Combine cucumber, onion, radishes, oil, vinegar, salt and remaining ¼ teaspoon pepper in small bowl; mix well.

3. Grill patties over medium heat, covered, 8 to 10 minutes (or 13 to 15 minutes uncovered) to medium (160°F) or to desired doneness, turning once. Top burgers with Cheddar cheese during last 2 minutes of grilling.

4. Place Gouda cheese on bottom halves of rolls; top with cucumber mixture, lettuce and burgers. Spread ketchup evenly on top halves of rolls; place on burgers.   *Makes 4 servings*

Audacious Two-Cheese Burger

Gourmet Burgers with Pancetta and Gorgonzola

1½ pounds ground beef chuck
2 ounces (about ½ cup) Gorgonzola or blue cheese crumbles
2 tablespoons mayonnaise
1 red bell pepper, quartered
4 thick slices red onion
   Salt and black pepper
4 egg or brioche rolls, split and toasted
   Oak leaf or baby romaine lettuce
4 to 8 slices pancetta or bacon, cooked until crisp

1. Prepare grill for direct cooking. Shape beef into 4 patties about ¾ inch thick. Cover and refrigerate. Combine cheese and mayonnaise in small bowl; refrigerate until ready to serve.

2. Grill bell pepper and onion over medium-high heat, covered, 8 to 10 minutes or until browned, turning once. (Use grill basket, if desired.) Transfer to plate; keep warm.

3. Grill patties over medium heat, covered, 8 to 10 minutes (or 13 to 15 minutes uncovered) to medium (160°F) or to desired doneness, turning once. Season with salt and black pepper.

4. Spread cheese mixture on cut sides of each roll. Place lettuce on bottom halves of rolls; top with burgers, pancetta, onion, bell pepper and top halves of rolls. *Makes 4 servings*

Zesty Chipotle Cheddar Burgers

2 pounds lean ground beef
2 cups medium salsa, divided
1 cup green onions, chopped and divided
1 cup tortilla chips, finely crushed and divided
1 tablespoon garlic salt
1 tablespoon chili powder
8 hamburger buns, split
8 slices SARGENTO® Deli Style Sliced Chipotle Cheddar Cheese

1. Combine ground beef, 1 cup salsa, ½ cup green onions, ½ cup tortilla chips, garlic salt and chili powder in large bowl. Shape beef mixture into 8 patties, 4 inches in diameter and ½ inch thick. Preheat grill or broiler.

2. Grill patties 5 minutes each side or until no longer pink in center (see Tip). Grill or lightly toast hamburger buns. Top patties with 1 slice cheese before removing from grill or broiler; let melt.

3. Place patties on buns. Top with remaining salsa, tortilla chips and green onions.   *Makes 8 burgers*

Cook Time: **10 minutes**

> ▌ TIP: For food safety, use a food thermometer to assure the internal temperature of the burgers is at least 160°F (the temperature of medium-done meat).

Deluxe Bacon & Gouda Burgers

1½ pounds ground beef chuck
⅓ cup mayonnaise
1 teaspoon minced garlic
¼ teaspoon Dijon mustard
4 thick red onion slices
  Salt and pepper
4 to 8 slices Gouda cheese
4 onion rolls, split and toasted
  Bibb lettuce leaves
  Tomato slices
4 to 8 slices bacon, cooked until crisp

1. Prepare grill for direct cooking. Shape beef into 4 patties about ¾ inch thick. Cover and refrigerate.

2. Combine mayonnaise, garlic and mustard in small bowl; mix well.

3. Grill patties and onion over medium-high heat, covered, 8 to 10 minutes (or 13 to 15 minutes uncovered) to medium (160°F) or to desired doneness, turning once. Remove onion when slightly browned. Season burgers with salt and pepper. Top burgers with cheese during last 2 minutes of grilling.

4. Place lettuce on bottom halves of buns; top with mayonnaise mixture, burgers, tomato, onion, bacon and top halves of rolls.

Makes 4 servings

Substitution: To save time, substitute a prepared mayonnaise spread for the garlic mayonnaise.

Deluxe Bacon & Gouda Burger

Ranchero Onion Burgers

  1 pound ground beef
½ cup salsa
½ cup (2 ounces) shredded Monterey Jack cheese
1⅓ cups *French's*® Cheddar or Original French Fried Onions, divided
½ teaspoon garlic powder
¼ teaspoon ground black pepper
  4 hamburger rolls

1. Combine beef, salsa, cheese, ⅔ *cup* French Fried Onions, garlic powder and pepper in large bowl. Shape into 4 patties.

2. Place patties on oiled grid. Grill* over medium coals 10 minutes or until no longer pink in center, turning once. Serve on rolls. Garnish with additional salsa, if desired. Top with remaining ⅔ *cup* onions.

Makes 4 servings

Or, broil 6 inches from heat.

Tip: For extra-crispy warm onion flavor, heat French Fried Onions in the microwave for 1 minute. Or, place in a foil pan and heat on the grill 2 minutes.

Tip: For Salsa Olé, combine 1½ cups prepared salsa with ¼ cup *Franks*® *Redhot*® Hot Sauce.

Prep Time: **10 minutes** | Cook Time: **10 minutes**

Ranchero Onion Burger

Brie Burgers with Sun-Dried Tomato and Artichoke Spread

½ cup sun-dried tomatoes packed in oil, drained
1½ pounds ground beef chuck
¼ cup chopped shallots
1 tablespoon plus 1 teaspoon minced garlic, divided
1 teaspoon black pepper, divided
½ teaspoon salt, divided
1 cup canned quartered artichokes, drained and chopped
2 tablespoons mayonnaise
¼ pound Brie, sliced
2 tablespoons butter, softened
4 egg or Kaiser rolls, split
   Heirloom tomato slices
   Arugula or lettuce leaves

1. Prepare grill for direct cooking. Chop sun-dried tomatoes.

2. Combine beef, half of chopped tomatoes, shallots, 1 tablespoon garlic, ½ teaspoon pepper and ¼ teaspoon salt in large bowl; mix lightly. Shape into 4 patties about ¾ inch thick. Cover and refrigerate.

3. Combine remaining half of chopped tomatoes, artichokes, mayonnaise, remaining 1 teaspoon garlic, ½ teaspoon pepper and ¼ teaspoon salt in small bowl; mix well. Season with salt, if desired.

4. Grill patties over medium heat, covered, 8 to 10 minutes (or 13 to 15 minutes uncovered) to medium (160°F) or to desired doneness, turning once. Top burgers with cheese during last 2 minutes of grilling.

5. Spread butter on cut sides of each roll. Toast or grill rolls until lightly browned. Spread artichoke mixture on bottom halves of rolls; top with tomato, burgers, arugula and top halves of rolls.   *Makes 4 servings*

Brie Burger with Sun-Dried Tomato and Artichoke Spread

The All-American Burger

Burger Spread (recipe follows)
1½ pounds ground beef
2 tablespoons chopped fresh parsley
2 teaspoons onion powder
2 teaspoons Worcestershire sauce
1 teaspoon garlic powder
1 teaspoon salt
1 teaspoon black pepper
4 hamburger buns, split
Lettuce leaves

1. Prepare grill for direct cooking. Prepare Burger Spread; set aside.

2. Combine beef, parsley, onion powder, Worcestershire sauce, garlic powder, salt and pepper in medium bowl; mix lightly. Shape into 4 patties about ¾ inch thick.

3. Grill patties over medium heat, covered, 8 to 10 minutes (or 13 to 15 minutes uncovered) to medium (160°F) or to desired doneness, turning once.

4. Serve burgers on buns with lettuce and Burger Spread.

Makes 4 servings

Burger Spread

½ cup ketchup
¼ cup mustard
2 tablespoons chopped onion
1 tablespoon relish or chopped pickles
1 tablespoon chopped fresh parsley

Combine ketchup, mustard, onion, relish and parsley in small bowl; mix well.

Makes 1 cup

The All-American Burger

Southwest Pesto Burgers

½ cup fresh cilantro, stemmed
1½ teaspoons chopped or sliced jalapeño pepper*
1 clove garlic
¾ teaspoon salt, divided
¼ cup vegetable oil
2 tablespoons mayonnaise
1¼ pounds ground beef
4 slices pepper jack cheese
4 Kaiser rolls
1 ripe avocado, sliced
Salsa

*Jalapeño peppers can sting and irritate the skin, so wear rubber gloves when handling peppers and do not touch your eyes.

1. Combine cilantro, jalapeño, garlic and ¼ teaspoon salt in food processor; process until garlic is minced. Slowly add oil with motor running; process until thick paste forms.

2. Prepare grill for direct cooking. Combine mayonnaise and 1 tablespoon pesto in small bowl; mix well.

3. Combine beef, remaining ¼ cup pesto and ½ teaspoon salt in large bowl; mix lightly. Shape into 4 patties.

4. Grill patties over medium heat, covered, 8 to 10 minutes (or 13 to 15 minutes uncovered) to medium (160°F) or to desired doneness, turning once. Top burgers with cheese during last 2 minutes of grilling.

5. Place burgers on bottom halves of buns; top with mayonnaise mixture, avocado, salsa and tops of buns.

Makes 4 servings

Southwest Pesto Burger

Beef and Mushroom Burger

1½ pounds extra-lean ground beef
1 small onion, minced
3 tablespoons fresh parsley
¼ cup light mayonnaise
1 tablespoon MRS. DASH® Tomato Basil Garlic Seasoning Blend
1 tablespoon Dijon mustard
6 portobello mushrooms
4 tablespoons MRS. DASH® Steak Grilling Blend™, divided
6 hamburger buns, split

1. Mix ground beef, onion and parsley in a bowl. Shape into 6 burgers.

2. Mix mayonnaise, MRS. DASH® Tomato Basil Garlic and mustard in a small bowl and set aside. Preheat grill to medium.

3. Remove stems from mushrooms and brush with water. Sprinkle with 1 tablespoon MRS. DASH® Steak Grilling Blend™. Place remaining MRS. DASH® Steak Grilling Blend™ on a plate and pat burgers into it on both sides.

4. Grill burgers and mushrooms, turning once, until mushrooms are browned and tender and the burgers reach 160°F.

5. Grill buns until toasted. Place each burger on a bun and top with a mushroom and reserved sauce.   *Makes 6 servings*

Prep Time: **10 minutes** | Cook Time: 15 to 16 minutes

Caesar Salad Beef Burgers on Garlic Crostini

1½ pounds ground beef
3 cloves garlic, minced
1 teaspoon salt
½ teaspoon pepper
4 Romaine lettuce leaves
¼ cup freshly shaved or grated Parmesan cheese

GARLIC CROSTINI

8 slices sourdough bread (about 4×3×½ inch)
Extra-virgin olive oil
2 large cloves garlic, cut lengthwise into quarters

1. Combine ground beef, minced garlic, 1 teaspoon salt and ½ teaspoon pepper in large bowl, mixing lightly but thoroughly. Lightly shape into four ¾-inch-thick patties, shaping to fit the bread slices.

2. Place patties on grid over medium, ash-covered coals. Grill, uncovered, 13 to 15 minutes (over medium heat on preheated gas grill, covered, 13 to 14 minutes) until instant-read thermometer inserted horizontally into center registers 160°F, turning occasionally. Season with salt and pepper, as desired.

3. Meanwhile, brush both sides of bread slices lightly with oil. Place bread around outer edge of grid. Grill a few minutes until lightly toasted, turning once. Remove bread slices from grid; rub both sides of each slice with a garlic quarter.

4. Place one lettuce leaf on four of the bread slices; top each with a burger. Sprinkle evenly with cheese; cover with remaining bread slices. Cut burgers in half; arrange on lettuce-lined platter, if desired.

Makes 4 servings

Tip: Use a vegetable peeler to quickly shave Parmesan cheese.

Prep and Cook Time: **30 minutes**

Favorite recipe courtesy of *The Beef Checkoff*

Backyard Barbecue Burgers

1½ **pounds ground beef**
⅓ **cup barbecue sauce, divided**
1 **onion, cut into thick slices**
1 to 2 **tomatoes, cut into slices**
1 to 2 **tablespoons olive oil**
4 **kaiser rolls, split and toasted**
    Green lettuce leaves

1. Prepare grill for direct cooking.

2. Combine ground beef and 2 tablespoons barbecue sauce in large bowl. Shape into 4 patties about 1 inch thick.

3. Grill patties over medium heat, covered, 8 to 10 minutes (or 13 to 15 minutes uncovered) to medium (160°F) or to desired doneness, turning occasionally. Brush both sides with remaining barbecue sauce during last 5 minutes of grilling.

4. Meanwhile, brush onion* and tomato slices with oil. Grill onion slices about 10 minutes and tomato slices 2 to 3 minutes.

5. Serve burgers on rolls with tomato, onion and lettuce.

Makes 4 servings

*Onion slices may be cooked in 2 tablespoons oil in large skillet over medium heat 10 minutes until tender and slightly brown.

Backyard Barbecue Burger

Grilled Reuben Burger

    1 envelope LIPTON® RECIPE SECRETS® Onion Soup Mix*
    ½ cup water
1½ pounds ground beef
    ½ cup shredded Swiss cheese (about 2 ounces)
    1 tablespoon crisp-cooked crumbled bacon or bacon bits
    ½ teaspoon caraway seeds (optional)

Also terrific with LIPTON® RECIPE SECRETS® Onion Mushroom Soup Mix.

1. In large bowl, combine all ingredients; shape into 6 patties.

2. Grill or broil until done. Top, if desired, with heated sauerkraut and additional bacon.   *Makes 6 servings*

Welsh Rarebit Pub Style Burgers

1½ pounds ground beef
    1 can CAMPBELL'S® Cheddar Cheese Soup
    ¼ cup water
    1 tablespoon Worcestershire sauce
    1 teaspoon prepared mustard
    6 English muffins, split and toasted

1. Shape beef into 6 patties, ½ inch thick.

2. Cook patties in a skillet until browned. Pour off fat.

3. Add soup, water, Worcestershire and mustard. Heat to a boil. Cover and cook over low heat 5 minutes or until done.

4. Serve on muffins with sauce.   *Makes 6 servings*

Prep and Cook Time: **20 minutes**

Grilled Reuben Burger

Beyond Beef

Chutney Turkey Burgers

1 pound ground turkey
½ cup prepared chutney, divided
½ teaspoon salt
½ teaspoon pepper
⅛ teaspoon hot pepper sauce
½ cup nonfat plain yogurt
1 teaspoon curry powder
4 hamburger buns, split

1. Preheat grill for direct-heat cooking.

2. In medium bowl, combine turkey, ¼ cup chutney, salt, pepper and hot pepper sauce. Shape turkey mixture into 4 burgers, approximately 3½ inches in diameter. Grill turkey burgers 5 to 6 minutes per side until 165°F is reached on meat thermometer and turkey is no longer pink in center.

3. In small bowl, combine yogurt, curry powder and remaining ¼ cup chutney.

4. To serve, place burgers on bottom halves of buns; spoon yogurt mixture over burgers and cover with top halves of buns.

Makes 4 servings

Favorite recipe from *National Turkey Federation*

Chicken Burgers with White Cheddar

1¼ pounds ground chicken
1 cup plain dry bread crumbs
½ cup diced red bell pepper
½ cup ground walnuts
¼ cup sliced green onions
¼ cup light beer
2 tablespoons chopped fresh parsley
2 tablespoons lemon juice
2 cloves garlic, minced
¾ teaspoon salt
⅛ teaspoon black pepper
4 slices white Cheddar cheese
4 whole wheat buns
   Dijon mustard
   Lettuce leaves

1. Combine chicken, bread crumbs, bell pepper, walnuts, green onions, beer, parsley, lemon juice, garlic, salt and black pepper in large bowl; mix lightly. Shape into 4 patties.

2. Spray large skillet with cooking spray; heat over medium-high heat. Cook patties 12 to 14 minutes or until cooked through (165°F), turning once. Top burgers with cheese. Cover skillet; cook about 1 minute or just until cheese melts.

3. Serve burgers on buns with mustard and lettuce. *Makes 4 servings*

Chicken Burger with White Cheddar

Deluxe Mediterranean Lamb Burgers

1½ pounds ground lamb
  1 tablespoon minced garlic
  2 teaspoons Greek seasoning
  1 teaspoon paprika
  ½ teaspoon salt, divided
  ½ teaspoon black pepper
  4 thin red onion slices, separated into rings
  1 tablespoon olive oil
  1 teaspoon chopped fresh mint or parsley
  1 teaspoon red wine vinegar
    Spinach leaves
  4 whole-grain rolls, split and toasted
  4 to 8 tomato slices
  1 package (4 ounces) feta cheese crumbles or Mediterranean feta cheese crumbles

1. Prepare grill for direct cooking.

2. Combine lamb, garlic, Greek seasoning, paprika, ¼ teaspoon salt and pepper in large bowl; mix lightly but thoroughly. Shape into 4 patties about ¾ inch thick. Cover and refrigerate.

3. Combine onion, oil, mint, vinegar and remaining ¼ teaspoon salt in small bowl; toss to coat.

4. Grill patties over medium heat, covered, 8 to 10 minutes (or 13 to 15 minutes uncovered) to medium (160°F) or to desired doneness, turning once.

5. Place spinach on bottom halves of rolls; top with burgers, tomato, onion mixture, feta cheese and top halves of rolls.   *Makes 4 servings*

Deluxe Mediterranean Lamb Burger

Barbecued Turkey Burgers

1 package JENNIE-O TURKEY STORE® Ground Turkey
¼ cup prepared barbecue sauce
2 tablespoons dry bread crumbs
4 whole grain sandwich buns

CLASSIC COLESLAW
2 cups thinly shredded cabbage
¼ cup *each* shredded carrot and thinly sliced red onion
3 tablespoons reduced-calorie mayonnaise
2 teaspoons *each* lime juice and granulated sugar

In medium bowl, combine turkey, barbecue sauce and bread crumbs; mix lightly. Shape into 4 patties (½ inch thick). Grill over hot coals, 4 inches from heat, until meat springs back when touched and burgers are no longer pink in center, about 4 minutes per side. Serve burgers topped with Classic Coleslaw in buns. *Makes 4 servings*

Classic Coleslaw: In large bowl, combine cabbage, carrot, onion, mayonnaise, lime juice and sugar. Mix well. Makes about 2½ cups.

Beyond Beef

Barbecued Turkey Burgers

Chicken Fajita Burgers

1 pound ground chicken
1 slice whole wheat bread, processed into crumbs
¼ cup chopped onion
2 tablespoons *each* chopped red and green bell pepper
2 tablespoons bottled medium-hot salsa
1 egg white, lightly beaten
1 tablespoon fajita seasoning
4 whole wheat hamburger buns, split, toasted
   Mexicali Mayonnaise (recipe follows)
4 lettuce leaves
4 tomato slices
8 avocado slices (thin vertical slices)

In a large bowl, mix together ground chicken, bread crumbs, onion, peppers, salsa, egg white and fajita seasoning. Form mixture into 4 patties. Place patties on rack of broiler pan. Position pan about 6 inches from heat and broil, turning once, 10 minutes or until burgers reach an internal temperature of 170°F. Spread cut side of bottom half of each toasted bun with 1 teaspoon Mexicali Mayonnaise. Top with lettuce, burger, tomato slice, 2 avocado slices, additional mayonnaise mixture, if desired, and top half of bun. *Makes 4 servings*

Mexicali Mayonnaise: In a small bowl mix 2 tablespoons light mayonnaise with 2 teaspoons bottled medium-hot salsa.

Favorite recipe from *Delmarva Poultry Industry, Inc.*

Bistro Burgers with Blue Cheese

1 pound ground turkey or beef
¼ cup chopped fresh parsley
2 tablespoons minced chives
¼ teaspoon dried thyme leaves
2 tablespoons *French's*® Honey Dijon Mustard
   Lettuce and tomato slices
4 crusty rolls, split in half
2 ounces blue cheese, crumbled
1⅓ cups *French's*® French Fried Onions

1. In large bowl, gently mix meat, herbs and mustard. Shape into 4 patties.

2. Grill or broil patties 10 minutes or until no longer pink in center. Arrange lettuce and tomatoes on bottom half of rolls. Place burgers on top. Sprinkle with blue cheese and French Fried Onions. Cover with top half of rolls. Serve with additional mustard.   *Makes 4 servings*

Tip: Toast onions in microwave 1 minute for extra crispness.

Prep Time: **10 minutes** | Cook Time: **10 minutes**

Savory Salmon Burgers

1 can (about 14 ounces) red salmon, drained
1 egg white
2 tablespoons toasted wheat germ
1 tablespoon dried onion flakes
1 tablespoon capers, drained
½ teaspoon dried thyme
¼ teaspoon black pepper
4 whole wheat buns, split and toasted
2 tablespoons Dijon mustard
4 tomato slices
4 thin red onion slices or dill pickle slices
    Lettuce leaves

1. Place salmon in medium bowl; mash with fork. Add egg white, wheat germ, onion flakes, capers, thyme and pepper; mix well.

2. Shape mixture into 4 patties. Cover and refrigerate 1 hour or until firm.

3. Spray large skillet with nonstick cooking spray. Cook patties over medium heat 10 minutes, turning once.

4. Spread cut side of each bun with mustard. Place burgers on bottom halves of buns; top with tomato, onion, lettuce and top halves of buns.

Makes 4 servings

> **TIP:** Red salmon is more expensive than pink salmon; it has a higher fat content, firm texture and deep red color.

Savory Salmon Burger

Grilled Salsa Turkey Burgers

½ **pound ground turkey**
2 **tablespoons salsa**
2 **tablespoons crushed tortilla chips**
2 **slices Monterey Jack cheese**
2 **whole wheat hamburger buns, split and toasted**
   Green leaf lettuce
   Additional salsa

1. Lightly spray grid with nonstick cooking spray. Prepare grill for direct cooking.

2. Combine turkey, 2 tablespoons salsa and chips in small bowl; mix lightly. Shape into 2 patties.

3. Grill patties over medium-high heat about 12 minutes or until cooked through (165°F), turning once. Top burgers with cheese during last 2 minutes of grilling.

4. Place lettuce on bottom halves of buns; top with burgers, additional salsa and top halves of buns. *Makes 2 servings*

Tip: To broil, preheat broiler. Broil burgers 4 to 6 inches from heat 6 minutes per side or until cooked through (165°F).

Grilled Salsa Turkey Burger

Cubano Burgers

1½ pounds ground pork
¼ cup minced green onions
3 tablespoons yellow mustard, divided
1 tablespoon minced garlic
2 teaspoons paprika
½ teaspoon black pepper
¼ teaspoon salt
8 slices Swiss cheese
4 bolillos or Kaiser rolls, split and toasted
8 slices sandwich-style dill pickles
¼ pound thinly sliced ham

1. Prepare grill for direct cooking.

2. Combine pork, green onions, 1 tablespoon mustard, garlic, paprika, pepper and salt in large bowl; mix lightly but thoroughly. Shape into 4 patties about ¾ inch thick, shaping to fit bread.

3. Grill patties over medium heat, covered, 8 to 10 minutes (or 13 to 15 minutes uncovered) to medium (160°F), turning once. Top burgers with cheese during last 2 minutes of grilling.

4. Spread remaining 2 tablespoons mustard on cut sides of each roll. Place pickles on bottom halves of rolls; top with burgers, ham and top halves of rolls. Press down firmly. *Makes 4 servings*

Note: Traditional Cuban sandwiches are made with sliced roast pork and do not include mayonnaise, tomatoes, onions, bell peppers or lettuce. Thinly sliced plantain chips usually accompany the sandwiches.

Substitution: A bolillo is an oval shaped roll about six inches long with a crunchy crust and a soft inside. If you can't find bolillos, use a loaf of French bread cut into individual-sized portions.

Cubano Burger

Turkey Burgers with Pesto-Red Pepper Mayonnaise

¼ cup HELLMANN'S® or BEST FOODS® Light Mayonnaise*
1 tablespoon prepared pesto
1 tablespoon finely chopped roasted red pepper
4 turkey burgers
4 Kaiser or whole grain rolls
  Tomato slices
  Lettuce leaves
  Onion slices (optional)

*Also terrific with HELLMANN'S® or BEST FOODS® Low Fat Mayonnaise Dressing or Canola Cholesterol Free Mayonnaise.

Combine HELLMANN'S® or BEST FOODS® Light Mayonnaise, pesto and roasted pepper in small bowl; set aside.

Grill or broil turkey burgers 8 minutes or until thoroughly cooked, turning once. To serve, evenly spread mayonnaise mixture on rolls, then top with burgers, tomato, lettuce, onion and dollop of mayonnaise mixture. *Makes 4 servings*

Prep Time: 10 minutes | Cook Time: 8 minutes

> ∎ **TIP:** To perk up the flavor of your burgers, mix WISH-BONE® Italian Dressing into the ground beef or ground turkey.

Turkey Burger with Pesto-Red Pepper Mayonnaise

Fired-Up Buffalo Burgers

1½ pounds ground turkey
¼ cup chopped green onions
1 teaspoon paprika
1 teaspoon salt
¼ teaspoon black pepper
½ cup hot pepper sauce
⅓ cup melted butter
1 cup shredded romaine lettuce
4 to 8 tomato slices (optional)
¾ cup blue cheese dressing, divided
¼ cup crumbled blue cheese
4 sesame seed buns, split and toasted
   Celery sticks (optional)

1. Prepare grill for direct cooking.

2. Combine turkey, green onions, paprika, salt and black pepper in large bowl; mix lightly. Shape into 4 patties about ¾ inch thick. Cover and refrigerate.

3. Combine hot pepper sauce and butter in small bowl; reserve ¼ cup mixture for dipping sauce.

4. Grill patties over medium heat, covered, 10 to 12 minutes or until cooked through (165°F), turning occasionally. Brush patties with hot sauce mixture during last 4 minutes of grilling, turning and brushing to coat both sides.

5. Place lettuce on bottom halves of buns; top with tomato, if desired, burgers, dressing, blue cheese and top halves of buns. Serve with celery sticks, if desired.   *Makes 4 servings*

Pork & Pepperoni Pizza Burgers

1 pound ground pork
½ cup (about 2 ounces) chopped pepperoni*
½ cup Italian-style dry breadcrumbs
½ cup prepared pizza sauce
½ teaspoon dried oregano leaves
6 sandwich buns
1 cup (4 ounces) shredded mozzarella cheese

*Try using a clean pair of scissors to cut pepperoni into small pieces.

In a medium bowl, stir together ground pork, pepperoni, bread crumbs, pizza sauce and oregano. Shape mixture into 6 patties. Grill or broil burgers for 5 minutes per side or until no longer pink inside. Place burgers on buns; top each patty with cheese. *Makes 6 servings*

Favorite recipe from *National Pork Board*

Apple Burgers

1 pound ground turkey breast
1 (16-ounce) jar MOTT'S® Apple Sauce, divided
2 tablespoons finely chopped onion
2 tablespoons finely chopped red or green bell pepper
¾ teaspoon salt
⅛ teaspoon ground white pepper
6 toasted buns

1. Spray broiler pan with nonstick cooking spray.

2. In large bowl, combine turkey, ½ cup apple sauce, onion, bell pepper, salt and white pepper; mix lightly. Shape mixture into 6 uniform patties. Arrange on prepared broiler pan.

3. Broil, 4 inches from heat, 5 minutes on each side or until lightly browned and no longer pink in center. Top each burger with remaining apple sauce; serve on buns. Refrigerate leftovers. *Makes 6 servings*

Mediterranean Australian Lamb Burger with Goat Cheese and Tomato Relish

BURGER

1¾ pounds Australian Lamb

1 shallot, peeled and chopped

1 tablespoon capers, chopped

6 to 8 large basil leaves, sliced

Freshly ground pepper, to taste

½ cup cornmeal (or flour), for coating

Olive oil, for cooking

TOMATO RELISH

3 vine-ripened tomatoes, halved crosswise

1 red onion, thickly sliced

1 teaspoon sugar

1 teaspoon balsamic vinegar

Salt and freshly ground pepper, to taste

PRESENTATION

4 Kaiser rolls or hamburger buns, split

4 tablespoons soft goat cheese (or chevre)

1. For burgers, combine ground lamb, shallot, capers, basil and pepper in a large bowl and mix well. Shape mixture into 4 burgers. Spread cornmeal over a plate and press burgers into cornmeal to coat.

2. Preheat barbecue grill or grill pan and brush with oil. Cook burgers over medium to high heat for 6 to 7 minutes or until internal temperature reaches 160°F.

3. For relish, place tomatoes flesh-side down on the grill and flip after 20 seconds, cooking until skin starts to char. Grill onions until soft; dice finely. Place in a bowl, add sugar and vinegar, season to taste with salt and pepper; mix well. Serve warm or cold.

4. Grill buns, cut side down, until lightly toasted. Spread with goat cheese and top with burgers. Serve with relish.   *Makes 4 burgers*

Favorite recipe from *Meat and Livestock Australia*

Mediterranean Australian Lamb Burger with Goat Cheese and Tomato Relish

Easy Salmon Burgers with Honey Barbecue Sauce

⅓ cup honey
⅓ cup ketchup
1½ teaspoons cider vinegar
1 teaspoon prepared horseradish
¼ teaspoon minced garlic
⅛ teaspoon crushed red pepper flakes (optional)
1 can (7½ ounces) salmon, drained
½ cup dried bread crumbs
¼ cup chopped onion
3 tablespoons chopped green bell pepper
1 egg white
2 hamburger buns, toasted

In small bowl, combine honey, ketchup, vinegar, horseradish, garlic and red pepper flakes until well blended. Set aside half of sauce. In separate bowl, mix together salmon, bread crumbs, onion, green pepper and egg white. Blend in 2 tablespoons remaining sauce. Divide salmon mixture into 2 patties, ½ to ¾ inch thick. Place patties on well-oiled grill, 4 to 6 inches from hot coals. Grill, turning 2 to 3 times and basting with remaining sauce, until burgers are browned and cooked through. Or place patties on lightly greased baking sheet. Broil 4 to 6 inches from heat source, turning 2 to 3 times and basting with remaining sauce, until cooked through. Place on hamburger buns and serve with reserved sauce.   *Makes 2 servings*

Favorite recipe from *National Honey Board*

Easy Salmon Burger with Honey Barbecue Sauce

BBQ Turkey Minis

½ cup panko bread crumbs
½ cup barbecue sauce, divided
1 egg, beaten
1 pound ground turkey
1 package (12 ounces) Hawaiian bread rolls, split horizontally
  Lettuce leaves
  Tomato slices
3 slices American cheese, quartered

1. Generously grease grid. Prepare grill for direct cooking.

2. Combine bread crumbs, ¼ cup barbecue sauce and egg in medium bowl; mix well. Add turkey; mix just until combined. Shape mixture by ¼ cupfuls into 12 patties about ½ inch thick.

3. Grill patties over high heat, covered, 8 to 10 minutes, turning once. Brush with remaining ¼ cup barbecue sauce during last minute of grilling.

4. Place lettuce on bottom halves of rolls; top with tomato, burgers, cheese and top halves of rolls. *Makes 12 mini burgers*

> ▌ **TIP:** The centers of turkey burgers should reach 160°F before being removed from the grill; the internal temperature will continue to rise to 165°F upon standing.

BBQ Turkey Minis

Lentil Burgers

1 can (about 14 ounces) vegetable broth
1 cup dried lentils, sorted and rinsed
1 small carrot, grated
¼ cup coarsely chopped mushrooms
1 egg
¼ cup plain dry bread crumbs
3 tablespoons finely chopped onion
2 to 4 cloves garlic, minced
1 teaspoon dried thyme
¼ cup plain yogurt
¼ cup chopped seeded cucumber
½ teaspoon dried mint
¼ teaspoon dried dill weed
¼ teaspoon black pepper
⅛ teaspoon salt
　Dash hot pepper sauce (optional)
4 rolls
　Lettuce leaves

1. Bring broth to a boil in medium saucepan over high heat. Stir in lentils; reduce heat to low. Simmer, covered, about 30 minutes or until lentils are tender and liquid is absorbed. Cool to room temperature.

2. Place lentils, carrot and mushrooms in food processor or blender; process until finely chopped but not smooth. (Some whole lentils should still be visible.) Stir in egg, bread crumbs, onion, garlic and thyme. Cover and refrigerate 2 to 3 hours.

3. Shape lentil mixture into 4 patties about ½ inch thick. Spray large skillet with nonstick cooking spray; heat over medium heat. Cook patties over medium-low heat about 10 minutes or until browned on both sides, turning once.

4. Meanwhile, for sauce, combine yogurt, cucumber, mint, dill, black pepper, salt and hot pepper sauce, if desired, in small bowl. Serve burgers on rolls with lettuce and sauce. *Makes 4 servings*

Portobello Mushroom Burgers

1 tablespoon olive oil, divided
¾ cup thinly sliced shallots
¼ cup mayonnaise
2 tablespoons chopped fresh basil
4 large portobello mushrooms, washed, patted dry and stems removed
¼ teaspoon salt
¼ teaspoon black pepper
2 cloves garlic, minced
4 whole-grain hamburger buns
4 ounces fresh mozzarella, cut into ¼-inch slices
2 jarred roasted red bell peppers, rinsed, patted dry and cut into strips

1. Heat 1 teaspoon oil in medium saucepan over medium heat. Add shallots; cook 6 to 8 minutes or until golden brown and soft, stirring occasionally. Meanwhile, combine mayonnaise and basil until well blended; set aside.

2. Preheat broiler. Line baking sheet with foil. Drizzle both sides of mushrooms with remaining 2 teaspoons oil; season with salt and black pepper. Place mushrooms cap side down on prepared baking sheet; sprinkle with garlic.

3. Broil mushrooms 4 minutes per side or until tender.

4. Spread cut sides of each bun with mayonnaise mixture. Divide cooked shallots and mozzarella slices evenly among bottom halves of buns; top with mushrooms, roasted peppers and top halves of buns.

Makes 4 servings

Portobello Mushroom Burger

Curried Walnut Grain Burgers

  2 eggs
⅓ cup plain yogurt
  2 teaspoons vegetarian Worcestershire sauce or soy sauce
  2 teaspoons curry powder
½ teaspoon salt
¼ teaspoon ground red pepper
1⅓ cups cooked couscous or brown rice
½ cup finely chopped walnuts
½ cup grated carrots
½ cup minced green onions
⅓ cup plain dry bread crumbs
  4 sesame seed hamburger buns
    Honey mustard
    Thinly sliced cucumber or apple

1. Spray grid with nonstick cooking spray. Prepare grill for direct cooking.

2. Combine eggs, yogurt, Worcestershire sauce, curry powder, salt and red pepper in large bowl; beat until blended. Stir in couscous, walnuts, carrots, green onions and bread crumbs. Shape mixture into 4 patties about 1 inch thick.

3. Grill patties over medium-high heat 10 to 12 minutes until browned, turning once. Serve burgers on buns with mustard and cucumber.

Makes 4 servings

Note: Burgers can be also broiled 4 inches from heat source 5 to 6 minutes per side or until done.

Curried Walnut Grain Burger

Black Bean Burgers

2 cans (about 15 ounces each) black beans, rinsed and drained, divided
¾ cup plain dry bread crumbs
⅔ cup coarsely chopped green onions
2 egg whites
¼ cup chopped fresh basil
2 teaspoons onion powder
2 teaspoons dried oregano
1 teaspoon baking powder
1 teaspoon ground cumin
1 teaspoon black pepper
½ teaspoon salt
¾ cup corn
¾ cup chopped roasted red pepper
6 whole wheat hamburger buns
   Salsa
   Avocado slices

1. Place half of beans in food processor; add bread crumbs, green onions, egg whites, basil, onion powder, oregano, baking powder, cumin, black pepper and salt. Pulse 30 to 40 seconds or until mixture begins to hold together. Fold in remaining beans, corn and roasted red pepper. Let stand 20 minutes at room temperature.

2. Preheat oven to 350°F. Line baking sheet with parchment paper.

3. Shape mixture into 6 patties (about ½ cup each). Place patties on prepared baking sheet; spray tops with nonstick cooking spray.

4. Bake 18 to 20 minutes or until firm. Serve burgers on buns with salsa and avocado.   *Makes 6 burgers*

Black Bean Burger

Middle Eastern Vegetable Grain Burgers

⅓ cup uncooked dried red lentils, sorted and rinsed
¼ cup uncooked brown or basmati rice
1 tablespoon olive oil
1 pound fresh mushrooms, sliced
1 medium onion, chopped
¾ cup grated Parmesan cheese
½ cup walnut halves, finely chopped
2 eggs
¼ cup chopped fresh cilantro
½ teaspoon black pepper
6 toasted sesame seed buns or toasted pita bread halves
  Mayonnaise
  Red onion slices
  Shredded lettuce
  Tomato slices

1. Place lentils in medium saucepan; cover with 1 inch water. Bring to a boil; reduce heat to low. Simmer, covered, 25 to 35 minutes or until tender. Rinse and drain; set aside. Meanwhile, cook rice according to package directions.

2. Heat oil in large heavy skillet over medium heat. Add mushrooms and chopped onion; cook and stir 20 to 25 minutes until mushrooms are brown. Combine mushroom mixture, cheese, walnuts, lentils, rice, eggs, cilantro and pepper in large bowl; mix well. Cover and chill.

3. Preheat broiler. Grease 15×10-inch jelly-roll pan with oil. Shape lentil mixture into 6 patties about ½ inch thick. Place patties on prepared pan.

4. Broil patties 4 inches from heat 6 to 8 minutes or until golden brown, turning once. Serve burgers on buns with mayonnaise, onion, lettuce and tomato. *Makes 6 servings*

Middle Eastern Vegetable Grain Burger

Beanie Burgers

    1 can (about 15 ounces) red kidney beans, rinsed and drained
    ½ cup chopped onion
    ⅓ cup quick oats
    1 egg
    1 tablespoon taco seasoning mix or mild chili powder
    ½ teaspoon salt
    4 slices cheese
    4 whole-grain hamburger buns, split and toasted
      Lettuce leaves
      Tomato slices
      Salsa, mayonnaise and/or mustard (optional)

1. Combine beans, onion, oats, egg, taco seasoning mix and salt in food processor. Pulse until mixture is blended and chunky, not smooth. (Mixture may be made up to 1 day in advance. Cover and refrigerate until needed.)

2. Spray large skillet with nonstick cooking spray; heat over medium heat. Spoon bean mixture into 4 round patties in skillet.

3. Cook patties 4 minutes on one side; turn carefully with spatula. Top burgers with cheese; cook 4 to 5 minutes.

4. Place lettuce on bottom halves of buns; top with burgers, tomato and top halves of buns. Serve with desired condiments.

Makes 4 servings

Beanie Burger

Chickpea Burgers

1 can (15 ounces) chickpeas, rinsed and drained
⅓ cup chopped carrots
⅓ cup herbed croutons
¼ cup chopped fresh parsley
¼ cup chopped onion
1 egg white
1 teaspoon minced garlic
1 teaspoon grated lemon peel
½ teaspoon black pepper
⅛ teaspoon salt
4 whole-grain hamburger buns
   Tomato slices, lettuce leaves and salsa

1. Place chickpeas, carrots, croutons, parsley, onion, egg white, garlic, lemon peel, pepper and salt in food processor; process until blended. Shape mixture into 4 patties.

2. Spray large nonstick skillet with nonstick cooking spray; heat over medium heat. Cook patties 4 to 5 minutes or until bottoms are browned. Spray tops of patties with cooking spray; turn and cook 4 to 5 minutes or until browned.

3. Serve burgers on buns with tomato, lettuce and salsa.

Makes 4 servings

Chickpea Burger

Portabella Mushroom Burgers

    REYNOLDS WRAP® Non-Stick Foil
3 tablespoons butter, melted
2 cloves garlic, minced
6 large portabella mushrooms
6 slices provolone cheese
6 hamburger buns

SAUCE

  1 cup light sour cream
  ¼ cup Dijon mustard
  2 tablespoons red wine vinegar
  2 teaspoons sugar
  ⅛ teaspoon cayenne pepper

PREHEAT grill to medium-high. Make drainage holes in a sheet of Reynolds Wrap Non-Stick Foil with a large fork; set aside.

COMBINE butter and garlic. Baste mushroom caps with mixture. Place foil on grill grate with non-stick (dull) side facing up. Immediately place mushrooms on foil.

GRILL uncovered 6 to 8 minutes, turning once, until mushrooms are browned and tender. Place 1 slice of cheese on each mushroom during the last minute of grilling.

COMBINE sour cream, mustard, vinegar, sugar and pepper in small microwave-safe bowl to make sauce. Microwave on HIGH power 30 seconds or until warm. Serve sauce over burgers in buns.

Makes 6 servings

Prep Time: 15 minutes | Grill Time: 6 minutes

Portabella Mushroom Burger

Stuffed Fiesta Burgers

1 pound ground beef
1 package (1¼ ounces) TACO BELL® HOME ORIGINALS®
    Taco Seasoning Mix
¼ cup PHILADELPHIA® Chive & Onion Cream Cheese Spread
⅓ cup KRAFT® Shredded Cheddar Cheese
4 hamburger buns, split, lightly toasted
½ cup TACO BELL® HOME ORIGINALS® Thick 'N Chunky
    Medium Salsa
1 avocado, peeled, pitted and cut into 8 slices

Preheat grill to medium heat. Mix meat and seasoning mix. Shape
into 8 thin patties. Mix cream cheese spread and shredded cheese.
Spoon about 2 tablespoons of the cheese mixture onto center of each
of 4 of the patties; top with second patty. Pinch edges of patties together
to seal.

Grill 7 to 9 minutes on each side or until cooked through (160°F).

Cover bottom halves of buns with burgers. Top with salsa, avocados
and top halves of buns.   *Makes 4 servings*

Prep Time: **15 minutes** | Grill Time: **9 minutes**

Mediterranean Burgers

1½ **pounds ground beef**
  2 **tablespoons grated Parmesan cheese**
  2 **tablespoons chopped kalamata olives**
  1 **tablespoon chopped fresh parsley**
  1 **tablespoon diced tomato**
  2 **teaspoons dried oregano**
  1 **teaspoon black pepper**
  4 **slices mozzarella cheese**
    Lettuce leaves
  4 **hamburger buns**

1. Prepare grill for direct cooking.

2. Combine beef, Parmesan cheese, olives, parsley, tomato, oregano and pepper in medium bowl; mix lightly. Shape into 4 patties about ½ inch thick.

3. Grill patties over medium heat, covered, 8 to 10 minutes (or 13 to 15 minutes uncovered) to medium (160°F) or to desired doneness, turning once. Top burgers with mozzarella cheese during last minute of grilling.

4. Place lettuce on bottom halves of buns; top with burgers and top halves of buns. *Makes 4 servings*

Serving Suggestion: For even more Mediterranean-inspired flavor, thinly slice bottled roasted red peppers and serve on burgers.

Mediterranean Burger

Curried Beef Burgers

1 pound ground beef
¼ cup mango chutney, chopped
¼ cup grated apple
1½ teaspoons curry powder
½ teaspoon salt
⅛ teaspoon black pepper
1 large red onion, sliced ¼ inch thick
4 Kaiser rolls or hamburger buns

1. Prepare grill for direct cooking. Combine beef, chutney, apple, curry powder, salt and pepper in medium bowl; mix lightly. Shape into 4 patties.

2. Grill patties over medium heat, covered, 8 to 10 minutes (or 13 to 15 minutes uncovered) to medium (160°F) or to desired doneness, turning once. Grill onion 5 minutes or until lightly charred, turning once. Serve burgers on rolls with onion.   *Makes 4 servings*

Classic Italian Burgers

1½ pounds lean ground beef
¼ cup WISH-BONE® Italian Dressing
¼ cup finely chopped green onions
2 tablespoons grated Parmesan cheese
2 large cloves garlic, finely chopped
4 hamburger buns
4 slices mozzarella or provolone cheese (optional)
   Lettuce and tomato slices (optional)

In medium bowl, combine ground beef, Wish-Bone Italian Dressing, green onions, Parmesan and garlic; shape into four ¾-inch-thick patties. Grill 13 minutes or until desired doneness, turning once. Serve on buns with mozzarella cheese, lettuce and tomato.   *Makes 4 servings*

Curried Beef Burger

East Meets West Burgers

1 pound ground beef (95% lean)
¼ cup soft whole wheat bread crumbs
1 large egg white
¼ teaspoon salt
⅛ teaspoon black pepper
4 whole wheat hamburger buns, split

SESAME-SOY MAYONNAISE

¼ cup light mayonnaise
1 tablespoon thinly sliced green onion, green part only
½ teaspoon soy sauce
¼ teaspoon dark sesame oil
⅛ teaspoon ground red pepper

SLAW TOPPING

½ cup romaine lettuce, thinly sliced
¼ cup shredded red cabbage
¼ cup shredded carrot
1 teaspoon rice vinegar
1 teaspoon vegetable oil
¼ teaspoon black pepper

1. Combine Sesame-Soy Mayonnaise ingredients in small bowl; refrigerate until ready to use.

2. Combine Slaw Topping ingredients in small bowl; set aside.

3. Combine ground beef, bread crumbs, egg white, salt and ⅛ teaspoon black pepper in large bowl, mixing lightly but thoroughly. Lightly shape into four ½-inch-thick patties.

4. Place patties on grid over medium ash-covered coals. Grill, covered, 11 to 13 minutes (over medium heat on preheated gas grill, covered, 7 to 8 minutes) until instant-read thermometer inserted horizontally into center registers 160°F, turning occasionally. About 2 minutes before burgers are done, place buns, cut sides down, on grid. Grill until lightly toasted.

continued on page 86

East Meets West Burger

5. Spread equal amount of Sesame-Soy Mayonnaise on bottom of each bun; top with burger. Evenly divide Slaw Topping over burgers. Close sandwiches. *Makes 4 servings*

Tip: To make soft bread crumbs, place torn bread in food processor or blender container. Cover; process, pulsing on and off, to form fine crumbs. One and one-half slices makes about 1 cup crumbs.

Prep and Cook Time: 30 to 40 minutes

Favorite recipe courtesy of *The Beef Checkoff*

Asian Turkey Burgers

 1 pound ground turkey
1⅓ cups *French's*® French Fried Onions, divided
 ½ cup finely chopped water chestnuts
 ¼ cup dry bread crumbs
 1 egg
 3 tablespoons Asian stir-fry sauce or teriyaki baste & glaze sauce
 1 tablespoon *French's*® *RedHot*® Original Cayenne Pepper Sauce
 2 teaspoons grated fresh ginger *or* ½ teaspoon ground ginger
 4 sandwich buns
  Shredded lettuce

1. Combine turkey, *1 cup* French Fried Onions, water chestnuts, bread crumbs, egg, stir-fry sauce, *Frank's*® *RedHot*® Sauce and ginger in large bowl. Shape into 4 patties.

2. Broil patties 6 inches from heat, or grill over medium coals, 10 minutes or until no longer pink in center, turning once. Serve on buns. Top with remaining ⅓ *cup* onions and lettuce.

 Makes 4 servings

Prep Time: 15 minutes | Cook Time: 10 minutes

Asian Turkey Burger

Greek Stuffed Burgers with Cucumber-Yogurt Sauce

1 (10-ounce) package frozen chopped spinach, thawed and
    squeezed dry
4 ounces (1 cup) feta cheese, crumbled
4 ounces (1 cup) sliced ripe olives
½ cup NEWMAN'S OWN® Balsamic Vinaigrette Salad Dressing
2 green onions, chopped
2 cloves garlic, minced
1 teaspoon dried oregano leaves
¾ teaspoon freshly ground black pepper, divided
1½ pounds lean ground beef
¼ teaspoon salt
    Cucumber-Yogurt Sauce (recipe follows)
    Lettuce leaves and tomato slices for garnish
4 whole wheat hamburger buns

With fork, mix spinach, feta cheese, olives, salad dressing, green onions, garlic, oregano and ½ teaspoon pepper. Set aside.

In medium bowl, mix ground beef with salt and remaining ¼ teaspoon pepper. Divide beef mixture into 8 equal portions; shape each into 3½-inch patty. Place heaping tablespoon of spinach mixture on 4 patties; top each with 1 remaining patty. Pinch edges of patties together to seal in spinach mixture.

Prepare Cucumber-Yogurt Sauce.

Lightly coat nonstick 12-inch skillet with olive oil spray. Heat skillet over medium heat; add burgers and cook 6 to 8 minutes, flipping halfway through cooking time, or until meat is cooked to desired doneness. Top burgers with remaining spinach mixture; cover skillet and cook 3 minutes. Serve burgers on buns garnished with tomato, lettuce and Cucumber-Yogurt Sauce. *Makes 4 servings*

Cucumber-Yogurt Sauce: In bowl, whisk together ½ cup plain low-fat yogurt, ½ small cucumber, peeled and finely chopped, and ¼ cup NEWMAN'S OWN® Balsamic Vinaigrette Salad Dressing.

Caribbean Beef Burgers with Mango Salsa

1 pound ground beef
2 teaspoons Caribbean jerk seasoning
Salt

MANGO SALSA

1 large mango, peeled, coarsely chopped (about 1 cup)
1 tablespoon chopped fresh cilantro
1 tablespoon chopped green onion
1 tablespoon finely chopped seeded jalapeño pepper
1 tablespoon fresh lime juice

1. Combine ground beef and jerk seasoning in large bowl, mixing lightly but thoroughly. Shape into four ¾-inch-thick patties.

2. Place patties on grid over medium ash-covered coals. Grill, covered, 13 to 15 minutes (over medium heat on preheated gas grill, covered, 13 to 14 minutes) until instant-read thermometer inserted horizontally into center registers 160°F, turning occasionally. Season with salt, as desired.

3. Meanwhile combine salsa ingredients in medium bowl, mixing lightly. Serve burgers with salsa. *Makes 4 servings*

Prep and Cook Time: **30 minutes**

Favorite recipe courtesy of *The Beef Checkoff*

> ▌ **TIP:** Burgers may be served open-face on thick slices of Hawaiian or Challah bread, if desired. Toast bread on the grill.

Polynesian-Style Burgers

    1 pound ground beef
    ¼ cup chopped onion
    ¼ cup chopped green bell pepper
    3 teaspoons soy sauce, divided
    ½ teaspoon ground ginger, divided
    ¼ teaspoon garlic powder
    1 can (5¼ ounces) pineapple slices
    4 herbed hamburger buns
      Lettuce leaves

1. Prepare grill for direct cooking. Combine beef, onion, bell pepper, 2 teaspoons soy sauce, ¼ teaspoon ginger and garlic powder; mix lightly. Shape into 4 patties.

2. Drain pineapple; reserve ¼ cup juice. Combine juice, remaining 1 teaspoon soy sauce and ¼ teaspoon ginger in pie plate. Add pineapple; turn to coat. Set aside.

3. Grill patties over medium heat, covered, 8 to 10 minutes (or 13 to 15 minutes uncovered) to medium (160°F) or to desired doneness, turning once.

4. Grill pineapple until heated through. Serve burgers on buns with pineapple slices and lettuce. *Makes 4 servings*

Polynesian-Style Burger

Velveeta® Wow! Burger

1½ pounds lean ground beef
6 ounces VELVEETA® Pasteurized Prepared Cheese Product,
   cut into 6 slices
6 whole wheat hamburger buns, toasted
1 can (10 ounces) RO*TEL® Diced Tomatoes & Green Chilies,
   drained

HEAT grill to medium heat. Shape meat into 6 (¾-inch-thick) patties.

GRILL 7 to 9 minutes on each side or until done (160°F). Top with VELVEETA®; grill 1 to 2 minutes or until melted.

PLACE cheeseburgers on bottom halves of buns; cover with tomatoes and tops of buns.   *Makes 6 servings*

Serving Suggestion: Serve with fresh fruit and assorted cut-up fresh vegetables to round out the meal.

How To Use Your Stove: Cook patties in skillet on medium heat 4 to 6 minutes on each side or until done (160°F). Top with VELVEETA®; cover with lid. Cook 1 to 2 minutes or until VELVEETA® is melted. Continue as directed.

Prep Time: 10 minutes | Total Time: 30 minutes

Blue Cheese Burgers

1¼ pounds ground beef
1 tablespoon finely chopped onion
1½ teaspoons chopped fresh thyme *or* ½ teaspoon dried thyme
¾ teaspoon salt
¼ teaspoon black pepper
4 ounces blue cheese, crumbled
4 whole wheat buns
Lettuce leaves, tomato slices and Dijon mustard

1. Prepare grill for direct cooking.

2. Combine beef, onion, thyme, salt and pepper in medium bowl; mix lightly. Shape into 8 patties. Sprinkle cheese in center of 4 patties to within ½ inch of edge; top with remaining patties. Press edges together to seal.

3. Grill over medium heat, covered, 8 to 10 minutes (or 13 to 15 minutes uncovered) to medium (160°F) or to desired doneness, turning once. Serve burgers on buns with lettuce, tomato and mustard.

Makes 4 servings

Spinach & Feta Burgers

2 pounds ground beef
½ cup water
4 ounces feta cheese, crumbled
1 package KNORR® Cream of Spinach Recipe Mix
1 tablespoon finely chopped garlic

In large bowl, combine all ingredients; shape into 8 patties. Grill or broil until done. Serve, if desired, on rolls with lettuce and tomato.

Makes 8 servings

Prep Time: 10 minutes | Cook Time: 12 minutes

Blue Cheese Burger

French Onion Burgers

1 pound ground beef
1 can (10½ ounces) CAMPBELL'S® Condensed French Onion Soup
4 slices Swiss cheese
4 round hard rolls, split

1. Shape the beef into 4 (½-inch-thick) burgers.

2. Heat a 10-inch skillet over medium-high heat. Add the burgers and cook until they're well browned on both sides. Remove the burgers from the skillet. Pour off any fat.

3. Stir the soup in the skillet and heat to a boil. Return the burgers to the skillet. Reduce the heat to low. Cover and cook for 5 minutes or until the burgers are cooked through. Top the burgers with the cheese and cook until the cheese is melted. Serve the burgers in the rolls with the soup mixture. *Makes 4 servings*

Kitchen Tip: You can also serve these burgers in a bowl atop a mound of hot mashed potatoes, with some of the onion gravy poured over.

Prep Time: **5 minutes** | Cook Time: **20 minutes**

French Onion Burger

Bacon Burgers

    8 slices bacon, cooked until crisp, divided
    1 pound ground beef
1½ teaspoons chopped fresh thyme *or* ½ teaspoon dried thyme
    ½ teaspoon salt
       Dash black pepper
    4 slices Swiss cheese
    4 Asiago rolls
       Lettuce leaves and red onion slices

1. Prepare grill for direct cooking.

2. Crumble 4 bacon slices. Combine beef, crumbled bacon, thyme, salt and pepper in medium bowl; mix lightly. Shape into 4 patties.

3. Grill patties over medium heat, covered, 8 to 10 minutes (or 13 to 15 minutes uncovered) to medium (160°F) or to desired doneness, turning once. Top burgers with cheese during last 2 minutes of grilling. Serve burgers on rolls with lettuce, onion and remaining bacon.

Makes 4 servings

Ragú® Pizza Burgers

    1 pound ground beef
    2 cups RAGÚ® Old World Style® Pasta Sauce, divided
    1 cup shredded mozzarella cheese (about 4 ounces), divided
    ¼ teaspoon salt
    6 English muffins, split and toasted

1. In small bowl, combine ground beef, ½ cup Ragú Pasta Sauce, ½ cup cheese and salt. Shape into 6 patties. Grill or broil until done.

2. Meanwhile, heat remaining pasta sauce. To serve, arrange burgers on muffin halves. Top with remaining cheese, sauce and muffin halves.

Makes 6 servings

Bacon Burger

Pace® Wild West Picante Burgers

1 pound ground beef
½ cup PACE® Picante Sauce or Chunky Salsa
4 PEPPERIDGE FARM® Classic Hamburger Buns, split

1. Thoroughly mix the beef and picante sauce in a medium bowl. Shape the mixture into 4 (½-inch-thick) burgers.

2. Lightly oil the grill rack and heat the grill to medium. Grill the burgers for 10 minutes or until desired doneness, turning them over halfway through grilling and brushing often with additional picante sauce.

3. Serve the burgers on the buns with additional picante sauce.

Makes 4 burgers

Serving Suggestion: Serve with coleslaw or fresh vegetables and ranch dressing for dipping and corn on the cob. For dessert, serve sliced watermelon or fresh fruit salad.

Prep and Cook Time: 15 minutes

Magically Moist Turkey Burgers

1¼ pounds ground turkey
½ cup finely chopped orange or red bell pepper
⅓ cup HELLMANN'S® or BEST FOODS® Real Mayonnaise
¼ cup plain dry bread crumbs
2 tablespoons finely chopped sweet onion
2 tablespoons finely chopped fresh parsley (optional)
½ teaspoon salt (optional)

In medium bowl, combine all ingredients; shape into 6 burgers. Grill or broil until done. Serve, if desired, on hamburger buns with your favorite toppings.

Makes 6 servings

Wild West Picante Burger

Lean Mean Cheeseburger

1 pound ground beef (95% lean)
2 tablespoons quick-cooking oats
½ teaspoon steak seasoning blend
4 seeded or whole wheat hamburger buns, split
4 slices lowfat cheese, such as Cheddar or American

TOPPINGS
Lettuce leaves, tomato slices (optional)

1. Place oats in foodsafe plastic bag. Seal bag securely, squeezing out excess air. Roll over bag with rolling pin to crush oats to a fine consistency.

2. Combine ground beef, oats and steak seasoning blend in large bowl, mixing lightly but thoroughly. Lightly shape into four ½-inch-thick patties.

3. Place patties on grid over medium, ash-covered coals. Grill, covered, 11 to 13 minutes (over medium heat on preheated gas grill, covered, 7 to 8 minutes) until instant-read thermometer inserted horizontally into center registers 160°F, turning occasionally.

4. Line bottom of each bun with lettuce and tomato, if desired; top with burger and cheese slice. Close sandwiches.   *Makes 4 servings*

Prep and Cook Time: **20 minutes**
Favorite recipe courtesy of *The Beef Checkoff*

Lean Mean Cheeseburger

Velveeta® Bacon Burgers

1 pound lean ground beef
2 tablespoons KRAFT® Light House Italian Reduced Fat Dressing
4 ounces VELVEETA® Pasteurized Prepared Cheese Product,
    cut into 4 slices
4 teaspoons OSCAR MAYER® Real Bacon Recipe Pieces
4 whole wheat hamburger buns, split

SHAPE ground beef into 4 patties. Cook in dressing in skillet on medium-high heat 10 to 12 minutes or until burgers are cooked through (160°F), turning after 5 minutes.

TOP with VELVEETA® and bacon; cover skillet with lid. Cook an additional 1 to 2 minutes or until VELVEETA® begins to melt. Serve in buns.   *Makes 4 servings*

Jazz It Up: Cover bottom half of each bun with lettuce leaf before topping with burger.

Cook Ground Meat Thoroughly: Cook ground beef thoroughly and evenly. The color of the raw ground meat can vary from bright red to light pink. Do not rely on the color of the meat to check for doneness but use an instant read thermometer instead. Ground beef should be cooked to an internal temperature of 160°F.

Serving Suggestion: Serve with bagged mixed greens tossed with cut-up fresh vegetables. Top with your favorite KRAFT® Dressing, such as Light Reduced Fat Ranch.

Prep Time: 10 minutes | Total Time: 24 minutes

Velveeta® Bacon Burger

Grilled Tri-Colored Pepper Salad

1 *each* large red, yellow and green bell pepper, cut into halves
    or quarters
⅓ cup extra-virgin olive oil
3 tablespoons balsamic vinegar
2 cloves garlic, minced
¼ teaspoon salt
¼ teaspoon black pepper
⅓ cup crumbled goat cheese (about 1½ ounces)
¼ cup thinly sliced fresh basil leaves

1. Prepare grill for direct cooking.

2. Place bell peppers, skin side down, on grid over high heat. Grill
bell peppers, covered, 10 to 12 minutes or until skin is charred. Place
charred bell peppers in paper bag. Close bag; set aside to cool 10 to
15 minutes. Remove skin; discard.

3. Place bell peppers in shallow glass serving dish. Combine oil, vinegar,
garlic, salt and black pepper in small bowl; whisk until well blended.
Pour over bell peppers. Let stand 30 minutes at room temperature.
(Or, cover and refrigerate up to 24 hours. Bring bell peppers to room
temperature before serving.)

4. Sprinkle bell peppers with cheese and basil just before serving.

Makes 4 to 6 servings

Veggie Salad with White Beans and Feta Cheese

1 medium green bell pepper, chopped
1 yellow bell pepper, chopped
1 can (14 ounces) quartered artichoke hearts, drained
1 cup grape tomatoes, halved (about 5 ounces total)
1 can (about 15 ounces) navy beans, rinsed and drained
¼ cup chopped fresh basil *or* 1½ tablespoons dried basil
    plus ¼ cup chopped fresh parsley
¼ cup extra-virgin olive oil
3 to 4 tablespoons red wine vinegar
1 clove garlic, minced
1 teaspoon Dijon mustard
½ teaspoon coarsely ground black pepper
¼ teaspoon salt
4 ounces crumbled feta cheese with sun-dried tomatoes and basil
4 cups (4 ounces) packed spring greens (optional)

1. Combine bell peppers, artichokes, tomatoes, beans, basil, oil, vinegar, garlic, mustard, black pepper and salt in large bowl; toss gently. Fold in feta cheese. Let stand 10 minutes.

2. Place greens on 4 serving plates, if desired. Top with vegetable mixture.

Makes 4 servings

Veggie Salad with White Beans and Feta Cheese

Lemony Cabbage Slaw with Curry

4 cups shredded green or white cabbage
2 tablespoons chopped green bell pepper
2 tablespoons chopped red bell pepper
1 green onion, thinly sliced
2 tablespoons cider vinegar
1 tablespoon lemon juice
1 tablespoon sugar
1 teaspoon curry powder
½ teaspoon salt
½ teaspoon celery seeds

1. Combine cabbage, bell peppers and green onion in large bowl. Whisk vinegar, lemon juice, sugar, curry powder, salt and celery seeds in small bowl. Pour over cabbage mixture; mix well.

2. Refrigerate, covered, at least 4 hours or overnight, stirring occasionally.
Makes 6 servings

> **TIP:** When purchasing green cabbage, look for well-trimmed, compact heads that feel heavy for their size. They should have a bright color and be free of withered, discolored or dry outer leaves.

Lemony Cabbage Slaw with Curry

Potato and Blue Cheese Salad

    8 new or fingerling potatoes (about 1 pound), scrubbed
½ teaspoon salt
½ cup shredded radicchio
¼ cup halved pitted kalamata or niçoise olives
¼ cup (1 ounce) crumbled Gorgonzola cheese
2½ tablespoons olive oil
  1 teaspoon white wine vinegar
  1 teaspoon Dijon mustard
¼ teaspoon black pepper

1. Place potatoes and salt in medium saucepan; add water to cover. Bring to a boil; cook 20 to 25 minutes or until tender. Drain well; cut into bite-size pieces.

2. Combine potatoes, radicchio, olives and blue cheese in large bowl. Blend oil, vinegar, mustard and pepper in small bowl. Pour over potato mixture; stir gently to coat. Let stand 30 minutes before serving.

Makes 4 servings

Potato and Blue Cheese Salad

BLT Salad with Bow Ties & Cheddar

2 cups (4 ounces) bow-tie or corkscrew-shaped pasta
1 package (9 ounces) DOLE® Organic Salad Blend Romaine
    & Radicchio or Baby Spinach Salad
1 cup cherry, pear or baby Roma tomatoes, halved
¾ cup (3 ounces) Cheddar cheese, diced
5 strips bacon, cooked, drained and crumbled *or* ⅓ cup packaged
    bacon bits
⅓ cup ranch salad dressing

• Cook pasta according to package directions. Drain well and rinse in cool water. Drain again.

• Toss together salad blend, pasta, tomatoes, cheese and bacon in large bowl. Pour dressing over salad; toss to evenly coat.

Makes 3 to 4 servings

Red Cabbage and Fruit Slaw

2 cups shredded savoy cabbage
⅓ cup shredded carrot
⅓ cup dried apricots, cut into thin matchstick strips
½ apple, cut into thin matchstick strips
½ cup mayonnaise
3 tablespoons cider vinegar
1 to 3 tablespoons sugar
2 cups shredded red cabbage

1. Combine savoy cabbage, carrot, apricots and apple in large bowl; mix well.

2. Combine mayonnaise, vinegar and sugar in small bowl until well blended. Pour over cabbage mixture; toss to coat. Refrigerate at least 1 hour before serving. Just before serving, stir in red cabbage.

Makes 6 to 8 servings

BLT Salad with Bow Ties & Cheddar

Spicy Orzo and Black Bean Salad

    4 tablespoons olive oil
    2 tablespoons minced jalapeño pepper,* divided
    1 teaspoon chili powder
    6 cups water
    ¾ cup uncooked orzo pasta
    1 cup frozen mixed vegetables
    1 can (about 15 ounces) black beans, rinsed and drained
    2 thin slices red onion, separated into rings
    ¼ cup chopped fresh cilantro
    ¼ cup fresh lime juice
    ¼ cup fresh lemon juice
    4 cups torn spinach leaves
    2 tablespoons crumbled blue cheese (optional)

Jalapeño peppers can sting and irritate the skin, so wear rubber gloves when handling peppers and do not touch your eyes.

1. Combine oil, 1 tablespoon jalapeño and chili powder in large bowl; set aside.

2. Bring water and remaining 1 tablespoon jalapeño to a boil in large saucepan. Add orzo; cook 10 to 12 minutes or until tender. Drain; rinse under cold water and drain again.

3. Place frozen vegetables in small microwavable dish. Cover and microwave on HIGH 3 minutes or until hot. Let stand 5 minutes.

4. Add orzo, vegetables, beans, onion, cilantro, lime juice and lemon juice to oil mixture; toss to coat. Divide spinach evenly among serving plates. Top with orzo mixture; sprinkle with blue cheese, if desired.

Makes 4 servings

Prep and Cook Time: **25 minutes**

Spicy Orzo and Black Bean Salad

Fruit Slaw

   1 package (16 ounces) coleslaw mix
   1 Granny Smith apple, cut into matchstick strips
   1 pear, cut into matchstick strips
   1 cup sliced strawberries
   ⅓ cup lemon juice
   2 tablespoons mayonnaise
   1 tablespoon sugar
   2 teaspoons poppy seeds
   1 teaspoon Dijon mustard
   ¼ teaspoon salt

1. Combine coleslaw mix, apple, pear and strawberries in large bowl.

2. Whisk lemon juice, mayonnaise, sugar, poppy seeds, mustard and salt in small bowl. Pour dressing over cabbage mixture; toss gently. Serve immediately. *Makes 7 cups*

Bayou Cajun Fries

   2 large baking potatoes, scrubbed
   4 teaspoons extra-virgin olive oil
   ½ teaspoon paprika
   ½ teaspoon seasoning salt
   ½ teaspoon Cajun seasoning

1. Preheat oven 475°F. Cut potatoes lengthwise into ¼-inch slices, then cut each slice into ¼-inch-wide strips. Place potatoes on baking sheet; drizzle with oil and sprinkle with paprika. Toss gently to coat. Arrange potato strips in single layer.

2. Bake 10 minutes; stir and bake 10 minutes more or until potatoes are golden brown and tender. Immediately sprinkle with salt and Cajun seasoning; toss gently to coat. *Makes 4 servings*

Fruit Slaw

South Asian Curried Potato Salad

  2 pounds new potatoes
1½ teaspoons salt, divided
  ¾ cup plain yogurt
  ½ cup diced onion
  ½ cup diced celery
  ⅓ cup diced green bell pepper
  ¼ cup mayonnaise
  2 teaspoons curry powder
  2 teaspoons lemon juice

1. Place potatoes and 1 teaspoon salt in large saucepan; add cold water to cover. Bring to a boil; boil 20 minutes or until just tender. Drain; cool to room temperature.

2. Combine yogurt, onion, celery, bell pepper, mayonnaise, curry powder, lemon juice and remaining ½ teaspoon salt in large bowl; mix well.

3. Cut small potatoes in half lengthwise; cut larger ones into 1-inch pieces. Add potatoes to yogurt mixture; stir gently to coat.

Makes 8 servings

South Asian Curried Potato Salad

Kohlrabi and Carrot Slaw

    2 pounds kohlrabi bulbs, peeled and shredded
    2 medium carrots, shredded
    1 small red bell pepper, chopped
    8 cherry tomatoes, cut into halves
    2 green onions, thinly sliced
    ¼ cup mayonnaise
    ¼ cup plain yogurt
    2 tablespoons cider vinegar
    2 tablespoons finely chopped fresh parsley
    1 teaspoon dried dill weed
    ½ teaspoon salt
    ¼ teaspoon ground cumin
    ⅛ teaspoon black pepper

1. Combine kohlrabi, carrots, bell pepper, tomatoes and green onions in medium bowl.

2. Combine mayonnaise, yogurt, vinegar, parsley, dill, salt, cumin and black pepper in small bowl until smooth. Add to vegetables; toss to coat. Cover and refrigerate until ready to serve.   *Makes 8 servings*

Sweet Potato Fries

    ½ teaspoon coarse salt
    ½ teaspoon *each* black and ground red pepper
    2 large sweet potatoes (about 8 ounces each)
    4 teaspoons olive oil

1. Preheat oven to 350°F. Combine salt and peppers in small bowl. Peel potatoes; cut lengthwise into long spears. Toss potatoes with oil on baking sheet until coated.

2. Arrange potatoes in single layer on baking sheet; sprinkle with salt mixture. Bake 45 minutes or until lightly browned.   *Makes 4 servings*

Kohlrabi and Carrot Slaw

Acknowledgments

The publisher would like to thank the companies and organizations listed below for the use of their recipes and photographs in this publication.

Australian Lamb

Courtesy The Beef Checkoff

Campbell Soup Company

Delmarva Poultry Industry, Inc.

Dole Food Company, Inc.

Jennie-O Turkey Store, LLC

©2010 Kraft Foods, KRAFT, KRAFT Hexagon Logo, PHILADELPHIA AND PHILADELPHIA Logo are registered trademarks of Kraft Foods Holdings, Inc. All rights reserved.

Mott's® is a registered trademark of Mott's, LLP

Mrs. Dash® SALT-FREE SEASONING BLENDS

National Honey Board

National Onion Association

National Pork Board

National Turkey Federation

Newman's Own, Inc.®

Reckitt Benckiser Inc.

Recipes courtesy of the Reynolds Kitchens

Sargento® Foods Inc.

Sonoma® Dried Tomatoes

Unilever

METRIC CONVERSION CHART

VOLUME MEASUREMENTS (dry)

1/8 teaspoon = 0.5 mL
1/4 teaspoon = 1 mL
1/2 teaspoon = 2 mL
3/4 teaspoon = 4 mL
1 teaspoon = 5 mL
1 tablespoon = 15 mL
2 tablespoons = 30 mL
1/4 cup = 60 mL
1/3 cup = 75 mL
1/2 cup = 125 mL
2/3 cup = 150 mL
3/4 cup = 175 mL
1 cup = 250 mL
2 cups = 1 pint = 500 mL
3 cups = 750 mL
4 cups = 1 quart = 1 L

VOLUME MEASUREMENTS (fluid)

1 fluid ounce (2 tablespoons) = 30 mL
4 fluid ounces (1/2 cup) = 125 mL
8 fluid ounces (1 cup) = 250 mL
12 fluid ounces (1 1/2 cups) = 375 mL
16 fluid ounces (2 cups) = 500 mL

WEIGHTS (mass)

1/2 ounce = 15 g
1 ounce = 30 g
3 ounces = 90 g
4 ounces = 120 g
8 ounces = 225 g
10 ounces = 285 g
12 ounces = 360 g
16 ounces = 1 pound = 450 g

DIMENSIONS

1/16 inch = 2 mm
1/8 inch = 3 mm
1/4 inch = 6 mm
1/2 inch = 1.5 cm
3/4 inch = 2 cm
1 inch = 2.5 cm

OVEN TEMPERATURES

250°F = 120°C
275°F = 140°C
300°F = 150°C
325°F = 160°C
350°F = 180°C
375°F = 190°C
400°F = 200°C
425°F = 220°C
450°F = 230°C

BAKING PAN SIZES

Utensil	Size in Inches/Quarts	Metric Volume	Size in Centimeters
Baking or Cake Pan (square or rectangular)	8×8×2	2 L	20×20×5
	9×9×2	2.5 L	23×23×5
	12×8×2	3 L	30×20×5
	13×9×2	3.5 L	33×23×5
Loaf Pan	8×4×3	1.5 L	20×10×7
	9×5×3	2 L	23×13×7
Round Layer Cake Pan	8×1½	1.2 L	20×4
	9×1½	1.5 L	23×4
Pie Plate	8×1¼	750 mL	20×3
	9×1¼	1 L	23×3
Baking Dish or Casserole	1 quart	1 L	—
	1½ quart	1.5 L	—
	2 quart	2 L	—